THE FRɛNCH COOKBOOK

Cécile de Dubois & René Bernard

Published by Mindful Publishing

TABLE OF CONTENT

TARTE FLAMBÉE

1171 kcal
Working time approx. 15 minutes
Rest period approx. 1 hour
cooking / baking time approx. 15 minutes
Total time approx. 1 hour 30 minutes

Ingredients
For the dough:
200 g flour
¼ cube yeast
¼ teaspoon sugar
¼ teaspoon salt
125 ml milk
For the flooring:
150 g bacon, smoked, lean, diced
150 g sour cream, or sour cream
1 medium-sized onion
1 tablespoon flour
2 tablespoons of oil

preparation
Prepare a yeast dough from flour, yeast, sugar, milk and salt and let it rise for about 20 minutes.

Halve the onion and cut into very thin strips. Mix sour cream, flour and oil with a whisk to a smooth cream and season with salt.

Roll out the dough in two portions on the floured work surface very thin. Place on a greased or baking paper-lined baking tray, spread with cream and sprinkle with onions and diced bacon. Bake in the oven preheated to 250 °C top/bottom heat for 12 - 15 minutes.

CRÊPES

1924 kcal
Working time approx. 15 minutes
cooking / baking time approx. 15 minutes
Total time approx. 30 minutes

Ingredients
250 g flour
500 ml milk
1 pinch of salt
1 package vanilla sugar
4 eggs
50 g butter

Preparation
Put the flour, milk, salt, vanilla sugar and eggs in a bowl and mix with a whisk. If the dough is too thick, add some more milk. Now melt the butter and stir it in as well (now best with an electric mixer).

Then brown briefly on both sides in the pan or on the crêpe pan.

Add a topping of your choice, fold up and serve immediately.

CHOCOLATE TART

4487 kcal
Total time approx. 30 minutes

Ingredients
200 g butter
100 g dark chocolate
150 g chocolate, whole milk
4 eggs
200 g sugar or powdered sugar
80 g flour
Grease for the mould
Powdered sugar to dust

Preparation
Melt the butter together with the chocolate in a pot. If you do it on a low flame with frequent stirring, no water bath is necessary.

Beat the eggs with the sugar until foamy. Sift the flour. Stir in the butter and chocolate mixture. Pour into a greased springform pan.

Bake in a preheated oven at 150 - 180°C for about 15 minutes. The cake will rise during baking and then collapse again.

The cake is ready when a few centimeters from the edge, when you try the toothpick, nothing remains to be tacked. It should not be completely through in the middle. The cake is super juicy, super delicious and in my opinion the only cake you can eat immediately after cooling down. Before serving, I dust it with powdered sugar.

BAGUETTE

3495 kcal
Working time approx. 40 minutes
Rest period approx. 1 day 4 hours
Total time approx. 1 day 4 hours 40 minutes

Ingredients
450 g wheat flour
450 g spelt flour
100 g rye flour
700 ml water, 9 degrees cold
20 g salt
15 g baking malt
20 g yeast, fresh

preparation
For 6 baguettes.

Poolish TA 200:
150 g French wheat flour type 65
150 g spelt flour 630
30 g rye flour 1150
330 g water (9°)
5 g yeast

Beat everything well so that there are no more

lumps in the dough and leave to mature for 12 hours at 24°.

Main dough TA 170:
300 g wheat flour type 65
300 g spelt flour 630
70 g rye flour 1150
370 g water (9°)
20 g salt
25 g baking malt
15 g yeast

Knead all the ingredients and the pre-dough in the spiral kneader for 20 minutes until the dough comes off the base. 30 minutes dough rest. Then fold it, put it in a larger bowl and put it in the fridge (5°) for 12 hours.

Then let it warm up for 1.5 hours. Form the baguette and put it in the oven for 1 hour. Cut into the baguette before shooting in. Bake at 240 degrees for 25 - 30 minutes.

TARTE AU CITRON

4153 kcal Working time approx. 30 minutes
Rest period approx. 4 hours
cooking / baking time approx. 25 minutes
Total time approx. 4 hours 55 minutes

Ingredients
For the dough:
200 g flour
100 g butter, soft
1 eggs
20 g almond, ground
75 g sugar
1 pinch of salt

For the cream:
3 lemon, untreated
3 eggs
2 egg yolks
100 g butter
120 g sugar
For the meringue: (Meringue)
2 egg white
1 pinch of salt
120 g sugar

Preparation
Recipe for a 28 tart

Dough:
Mix the soft butter with the sugar to a creamy mixture. Add salt and the egg and mix well. Then add the flour and the ground almonds and knead to a homogeneous dough. Put the dough in cling film for 1 hour in the refrigerator.

Line a tart mould with the dough, prick it slightly with a fork and cover with baking paper. Dried pulses (e.g. peas) can also be used to prevent the dough from forming bubbles or bulging during baking. Bake in the oven for 10 min at 180°C. Then remove the baking parchment or pulses and put them in the hot oven for another 10 minutes, so that the dough becomes nice and cookie-dry. Then let the baked dough cool down in the form.

Lemon cream:
Cut the peel of the lemons into zests and chop them finely. Cook about 115 ml lemon juice with the chopped zests for 3 minutes in a pot. Remove the pot from the heat and add butter, sugar, eggs and egg yolks to the pot and mix. Heat the cream over medium heat while stirring until it begins to thicken. This can take about 10-15 minutes. The cream will then quickly become very thick and you pour it onto the bottom of the pastry. I then always put the tart in the fridge for a few hours so that it can cool

down nicely.

Meringue:
Whip the eggs, salt and sugar and decorate the tarte au citron with a piping bag. Place the tarte au citron in the oven under the grill until the meringue turns a nice brown color.

TARTE AUX POMMES

2230 kcal
Total time approx. 20 minutes

Ingredients
200 g flour
100 g butter, room temperature
1 tablespoon of sugar
1 pinch of salt
5 thick apples
2 tablespoons of sugar
some vanilla, or cinnamon
Lemon juice

Preparation
Knead flour, butter, 1 tablespoon sugar and a pinch of salt. Then form into a smooth dough ball with half a glass of water. Put it in a cool place.

Then prepare a compote of apples. Peel 2 apples and cut them into small pieces. Heat them in a pot with 2 tablespoons of sugar, possibly some lemon juice and the pulp of a vanilla pod or a teaspoon of cinnamon powder. After about 15 minutes simmer on low heat (or 8 minutes in the microwave) and puree to apple-sauce with a hand blender.

Roll out the dough and lay it out in a 26 cm diameter tart tin, which is either covered with baking paper or buttered and floured. Prick small holes with a fork.
Peel the remaining 3 apples and cut into thin slices. First spread the apple compote on the dough, then spread the apple slices tightly on top. Bake at 200°C for 30 minutes.

TARTE FLAMBÉE WITH GOAT CHEESE, ROSEMARY AND HONEY

Working time approx. 20 minutes
cooking / baking time approx. 20 minutes
Total time about 40 minutes

Ingredients
For the dough:
200 g flour
2 tablespoons of oil
125 ml water
1 teaspoon salt
For the flooring:
200 g heavy cream
200 g onion
200 g soft goat cheese

3 tablespoons rosemary, fresh, finely chopped
2 tablespoons honey, liquid

Also:
Grease for the baking tray

Preparation
For the dough, mix the flour, oil, water and salt to a smooth, non-sticky dough, add some more flour. Roll out the dough thinly on a greased baking tray.

Lightly salt the Crème Double and pour it onto the dough. Cut the onions into very thin rings and spread on the dough. Cut the goat's cheese into thin slices and also lay them on the dough. Then sprinkle the rosemary leaves over it.

Bake the tarte flambée on the highest heat for 15 - 20 minutes until the edge is nicely brown and the cheese begins to melt.

After baking, pour the liquid honey with a spoon in a thin stream over the cheese or serve it separately. Serve hot immediately.

ORANGE MARMALADE

1682 kcal
Working time approx. 40 minutes
Rest period approx. 2 days
cooking / baking time approx. 2 hours
Total time approx. 2 days 2 hours 40 minutes

Ingredients
6 organic oranges
1.8 liters of water, per kilo of fruit
650 g jam sugar 2:1 or 1.3 kg jam sugar 1:1 per kilo
fruit mass

Preparation
Carefully wash organic oranges with edible peel.

Cut off the orange butt and head, then cut as finely
as possible with the peel. If necessary, put it through
the slicer of the food processor.
Remove the seeds as good as possible and store them
in a bag, tie it up, I always use the paper tea filters for
this.

Weigh this fruit mass, add 1.8 liters of water per kilo of fruit. Put the fruits with the water and the bag of seeds in a bowl and let it cool for 24 hours.

After the 24 hours, bring the whole mass to the boil in a pot, let it simmer for about 1 hour. Then leave to stand in a cool place for another 24 hours.
Then remove the core bag and squeeze out well.

Weigh the whole mass again, add 1.3 kg of 1:1 preserving sugar or 650 g of 2:1 preserving sugar per kg of fruit mass. I myself always take jam sugar 1:2. 1:3 sugar is almost not sweet enough in my opinion. Depending on how many or few seeds the oranges have contained, increase the amount of sugar slightly.

Then bring everything to the boil and let it boil for 1 hour, then fill it into hot, clean glasses and close the glasses.

TARTE WITH PÂTE BRISÉE AND EGG CREAM FILLING

Working time approx. 30 minutes
cooking / baking time approx. 40 minutes
Total time approx. 1 hour 10 minutes

Ingredients
125 g butter
250 g flour
70 ml water 80 ml
4 eggs
150 g sugar
500 ml sweet cream
60 Corn starch
1 big tin of fruit if desired (e.g. pears, mirabelle plums, peaches, ...)

Preparation
During a short trip to Alsace I was allowed to taste a gigantic cake as dessert. Here is the recipe I got from the cook herself (in French)

First, make a compact but smooth short pastry with 125 g butter (soft, room temperature), 250 g flour and about up to (rather less) 80 ml water. Put it in a cold place while you make the filling.

For the filling, whisk the 4 eggs with 150 g sugar and then add 1/2 liter cream and 60 g cornstarch.

When the filling is ready, you can take the dough out of the refrigerator and press it into a tart tin, alternatively a large round pizza tray or a large springform pan. In doing so, form a firm and as dense as possible rim about 3 - 4 cm high. This will later ensure that the (initially very liquid) filling does not overflow. If the dough is still too soft, leave it in the refrigerator a little longer! Prick a few holes in the bottom of the dough with a fork and fill in the filling.

If you would like to bake fruit as desired, cover the dough with the fruit pieces (fresh or canned, I have already tried mirabelle plums, pears and peaches, they were always delicious!) Put them on the middle shelf in the oven preheated to about 200 degrees! A pre-baking of the short pastry was not necessary for me so far, but it worked!

TIP: Since the egg cream filling is very liquid, and you have a problem getting it to the oven, I put the mold with the dough on a grid in the middle shelf of the oven and then poured the egg cream into it!

I usually baked the tart for about 50 minutes, you

should check it more often until the filling is completely solid (it is no longer liquid and doesn't slosh when the mould is moved). If the surface should brown too much, you can cover it with aluminium foil.

Cut the cooled tart into rather narrow pieces (16 - 20) as it is very rich and satiating because of the cream, but incredibly tasty!

Have fun baking the cake!

BRETON
APPLE PIE

Total time approx. 30 minutes

Ingredients
150 g butter
4 eggs
150 g sugar
2 cl Calvados
1 pinch of salt
150 g flour
1 knife point of baking powder
500 g apples, peeled, cored, cut into slices
Powdered sugar, mixed
Vanilla sugar

Preparation Melt butter, let it cool down a little. Beat eggs, sugar, calvados and salt until fluffy, stir in butter. Mix flour and baking powder and stir in. Preheat oven to 200°. Mix 400 g apple slices into the dough and fill into a greased springform pan. Spread 100 g apple slices rosette-like on the dough.

Bake the cake on the lowest ledge at 180°C for 40 -

50 minutes. Cover after 25 minutes. At the end of the baking time (make a stick test, bake for a few more minutes if necessary!) remove the cake from the springform pan and let it cool down on a rack. Sprinkle with a mixture of icing sugar and vanilla sugar.

With a scoop of vanilla or walnut ice cream, this cake is also very suitable for dessert.

FRENCH YOGHURT - NUT CAKE

Working time approx. 15 minutes
cooking / baking time approx. 1 hour
Total time approx. 1 hour 15 minutes

Ingredients
4 eggs
1 cup of hazelnuts, ground
1 ½ cup of sugar, up to 2 cups at will
2 cups of flour
1 cup of oil
1 shot of rum
150 g natural yoghurt
1 package baking powder
1 package vanilla sugar
Fat and breadcrumbs for the mould

Preparation
The cup used as a measure holds 250 ml.

Grease a 26-piece baking tin with oven base and

sprinkle with breadcrumbs. Preheat the oven to 160°C.

Place all ingredients in a bowl and mix with a hand mixer (approx. 3-5 minutes). Fill the dough into the baking tin and bake for about 1 hour.

CASSIS - LIQUEUR

231 kcal
Total time approx. 30 minutes

Ingredients
1 kg currants, black
1 liter of schnapps (grain, fruit schnapps, brandy)
1 vanilla pod
1 piece of ginger
500 g sugar (rock candy)

Preparation
Wash the currants well and drain. Then put them into a wide-necked glass, add the spices, sugar and brandy. Make sure that the glass is well closed.
Store in the dark for two weeks. Then filter and fill the cassis into bottles.
Cassis loves dark and cool storage.
The black currant is a small vitamin bomb, especially rich in vitamin C, but also B. It provides magnesium, calcium, phosphorus, iron, zinc, manganese and iodine.

CANNELÉS BORDELAIS

2379 kcal
Working time approx. 15 minutes
Rest period approx. 1 day
Total time approx. 1 day 15 minutes

Ingredients
½ liters of milk
250 g powdered sugar (normal sugar is also possible)
2 medium-sized eggs
2 egg yolks
5 cl rum
1 vanilla pod, scraped out pulp
100 g flour
40 g butter
1 pinch of salt

Preparation
Mix sugar, flour and salt together. Lightly whisk the eggs and the egg yolks with a fork and add to the mixture. Bring the milk with the vanilla pulp and butter to the boil and slowly add to the sugar-flour mix-

ture, stirring constantly. When the dough is luke-warm, add the rum. The dough is very liquid, but this is normal. Keep the dough cold for 24 hours. It can be kept in the refrigerator for 2 to 3 days.

Fill silicone moulds to 5 mm under the rim. Bake in the oven preheated to 240° for 10 minutes. Then turn the heat down to 190° and bake for another 30-40 minutes. I bake them for 30 minutes and leave them in the oven for 10 minutes with the heat off.

Let the ramekins cool down. Enjoy the tartlets luke-warm.

ONION TART

5785 kcal
Working time approx. 30 minutes
Rest period approx. 1 hour
Total time approx. 1 hour 30 minutes

Ingredients
500 g flour
50 g butter
¼ Liters of milk
1 package yeast
1 teaspoon of sugar
1 teaspoon of salt
For the flooring:
1 kg onion
80 g butter
1 tablespoon flour
2 eggs
3 tablespoons of milk
200 g bacon, smoked
Caraway, ground
⅛ Liters of sour cream
2 egg yolks
500 g cheese, Gouda (grated)

Preparation

Dissolve the yeast in the lukewarm milk with the sugar. Add the butter in small flakes to the flour. Add the yeast mixture and finally the salt.

Knead all the ingredients well together to form a smooth dough.

Place the dough on a greased baking tray and roll out evenly. Leave to rise in a non-heated oven for about 1/2 hour.

In the meantime, halve the onions and cut into fine rings. Sauté in approx. 80 g butter, but DO NOT brown. Add the bacon cut into fine cubes and fry briefly. Depending on the liquid that the onions give off, dust with approx. 1 tbsp. flour to bind them.

Mix 2 eggs with 3 tbsp. milk and season with some ground caraway. Add to the onions. Spread everything evenly on the dough.

PRE-Bake for 15 minutes at 200°C - 225°C on the middle shelf.

In the meantime mix 1/8 l sour cream, 2 egg yolks and 500 g grated Gouda. Spread evenly on the pre-baked cake and bake for another 30 minutes at 170°C.

The cheese crust should be golden yellow and the underside of the dough slightly browned - then the onion cake is just right.

Goes well with lamb's lettuce or other greens and Federweisser or a palatable white wine.

YEAST SNAIL CAKE

3317 kcal
Working time approx. 30 minutes
Rest period approx. 2 hours 30 minutes
cooking / baking time approx. 40 minutes
Total time about 3 hours 40 minutes

Ingredients For the dough:
500 g flour
1 teaspoon of salt
50 g sugar
70 g butter, soft
1 eggs
1 package vanilla sugar
100 ml milk, lukewarm
100 ml water, lukewarm
24 g yeast
For the filling:
350 ml milk
1 pinch of salt
3 tablespoons of sugar
1 package of custard powder

1 egg yolk, for spreading

Preparation
I personally never make a pre-dough, because I always succeed wonderfully without it and therefore I do not need it. But if you want to make one, you are welcome to do it the way you know it best.

Mix milk with water and dissolve yeast together with sugar and salt.
Put aside for a moment. Knead the flour and soft, but not too liquid butter briefly. Add the yeast milk and the egg and knead for at least 10 minutes, either with the machine or with your hands, as long as the kneading time is long enough for the dough to come off the bowl. Cover and let rest for at least 1-2 hours until the dough has increased its volume. (Of course, you can also have it all prepared in the BBA).

Meanwhile, prepare the pudding with the indicated ingredients as you know it!
Let it cool down covered, best is to stir it in between, so that no skin is formed!

After resting or walking, whip the yeast dough again vigorously and knead well.

Roll out the dough on a floured work surface to a thickness of about 1cm to a rectangle of about 60x40cm and spread with the pudding. Now roll up the dough and cut it into slices, so to speak into snails! The slices should be about 4-5 cm thick. (Caution! makes a huge mess through the pudding)

Now place them in a springform pan, press them slightly flat and let them go for another 30 minutes until their volume has increased significantly.
Brush the snails with an egg yolk if you like it.

Place the oven on 180°C top/bottom heat or 160°C circulating air and place the springform pan in the middle of the oven.
Bake the snails for about 35-40 minutes until golden brown.
If they get too dark, they are already done, please be careful, because every oven is different.
With me they need only 35 minutes.

Let them cool down well and then serve.

The snail cake is very juicy and different from the usual snails.

You can also use a cinnamon-sugar-butter mixture instead of pudding powder or something fruity, there are no limits.

MACARONS

1602 kcal
Working time approx. 20 minutes
Rest period approx. 50 minutes
cooking / baking time approx. 15 minutes
Total time about 1 hour 25 minutes

Ingredients
90 g egg white, from about 3 eggs
25 g sugar
1 pinch of salt
110 g ground almond
200 g powdered sugar

Preparation
Sift powdered sugar and ground almonds together in a bowl and mix. It is best to sift everything 2 to 3 times.
Beat the egg white and salt and let the sugar slowly trickle in. Now beat the egg white until it is firm.

Now slowly fold in the icing sugar-almond mixture. It should be a shiny, viscous mass.

Pour the mixture into a piping bag with a large perforated spout and squirt circles onto a baking tray covered with baking paper. Leave space between the circles.

Now let the macarons dry for 50 minutes. Then put all baking trays in the oven at the same time and bake at 140°C for about 15 minutes.

After baking, let the macarons cool down and put them into a sealable tin for 24 hours. Afterwards they can be filled with ganache, buttercream etc. and placed on top of each other.

It is best to fix the baking paper with butter on the baking tray so that it does not flutter. You can also weigh it down with cutlery.

This is the first macaron recipe where I succeeded in making macarons. You just have to follow the recipe exactly.

Makes about 25 pieces.

APPLE TART

3453 kcal
Working time about 35 minutes
Rest period approx. 8 hours
Total time approx. 8 hours 35 minutes

Ingredients
200 g flour
¼ teaspoon salt
130 g butter, ice cold
Water, ice cold
Flour, for work
1 kg apples (Boskoop)
½ Lemon, juice thereof
100 g sugar
Butter, for the mould
1 egg white
1 egg yolk
2 ½ Tablespoons of butter

Preparation
For a 28 cm diameter mould.
Sift the flour into a bowl and mix with the salt. Turn the ice-cold butter briefly in the flour and grate into the flour on the cheese grater. Gradually add ice-

cold water and squeeze the mixture together again and again. Do not knead under any circumstances. Always add just enough water to allow the dough to form. Shape into a ball and leave to rest in the refrigerator for at least two hours, preferably overnight.

Peel apples, remove seeds and cut into 1/2 cm wide slices. Put them in a bowl and sprinkle with lemon juice. Pour half of the sugar over it and let it stand for 1 hour. Then drain in a sieve over a bowl. Pick up the apple marinade and mix with the egg yolk.

Preheat the oven to 250°. Butter a tart tin or springform pan.
Knead the dough gently on a floured surface and roll out thinly. Put it into the form, press the rim a little bit. Brush the dough with egg white. Place the apple slices in a circle in the form. Sprinkle the remaining sugar over them and spread the butter on top.

Place the mould on the bottom of the oven. After 5-10 minutes, when the rim turns brown, put it on the middle shelf of the oven and bake for another 10 minutes. Spread the tart with the egg yolk and apple marinade and bake for another 10-15 minutes. The tart should have a golden brown crust. Let it cool down a little bit and take it out of the tin, eat it lukewarm.

Vanilla ice cream goes very well with it.

QUATRE QUARTS

Total time about 10 minutes

Ingredients
3 eggs
Flour
Sugar
Butter
1 package baking powder
Cake glaze of chocolate or powdered sugar with lemon

Preparation
Weigh the eggs. For sugar, butter and flour, weigh the same weight as the three eggs. Make a sponge mixture and add the baking powder. Pour into a greased springform pan and bake at 150 degrees for about 50 minutes.

If you wish, you can also cover the cake with chocolate or lemon icing (made of powdered sugar and lemon juice).

NECTARINES
- ROSES -
LAVENDER - TART

Total time approx. 20 minutes

Ingredients
160 g flour
1 teaspoon of salt
1 tablespoon of sugar
100 g butter, cold, diced
½ cup of ice - water
5 nectarine
5 tablespoons of jam (rose, but apricot, currant or strawberry jam also works)
2 teaspoons flowers, (lavender flowers)

Preparation
Sieve the flour, salt and sugar into a bowl and then work the butter into the flour with 2 knives or a Pastrycutter. Then knead the dough and add only as much water as necessary to obtain a smooth dough. Put the dough in foil in the fridge for 30-45 minutes.

In the meantime, stone and slice the nectarines. Heat and melt the jam.
Butter a tart mould or small moulds and preheat the oven to 190°C.

Roll out the dough and press it into the form. Arrange the nectarines nicely on the dough. Sprinkle some lavender blossoms over them and then pour the jam over them.

Bake for about 35 - 45 minutes until the dough is crispy golden brown. Let it cool down and serve with whipped cream or ice cream

GRENOBLE NUT COOKIES

Working time approx. 30 minutes
Total time approx. 30 minutes

Ingredients
For the dough:
120 g flour
50 g sugar
70 g hazelnuts, grated
1 pinch of salt
1 pinch of cinnamon
½ Lemon, unsprayed, grated peel
1 eggs, including the yolk
80 g butter, cold
For the flooring:
1 eggs, including the egg white
60 g sugar
50 g hazelnuts, grated
40 Hazelnuts

Preparation
Make short pastry. Form the dough into a roll of ap-

prox. 4 cm diameter, wrap in foil and let it rest in the refrigerator for at least 30 minutes. Preheat the oven to 200° C.

Beat egg white until frothy, add sugar and continue beating until the beaten egg white is firm. Add the ground nuts to the beaten egg white.

Cut the dough roll into 40 slices of equal thickness, place them on the baking tray covered with baking paper, spread with the meringue mixture and place 1 hazelnut in the middle of each cookie.

Bake in the middle shelf of the oven for 12 to 15 minutes until golden brown.

GALETTE DES ROIS À LA FRANGIPANE

678 kcal
Working time approx. 25 minutes
Rest period approx. 1 hour
Total time about 1 hour 25 minutes

Ingredients
400 g puff pastry, 2 circles, each Ø 30cm
125 g powdered sugar
125 g almond, finely grated
100 g butter, soft
2 eggs, whisked
1 egg yolk, whisked
2 tablespoons rum, dark
1 tablespoon aroma (almond essence)

Preparation
Blanch the finely grated almonds in a pan with a little butter, stirring constantly. Place in a bowl and allow to cool.

Add the powdered sugar and mix.

Whip the butter in another bowl, fold in the almond mixture and add the eggs, rum and almond essence and work well. Chill for half an hour.

Place a circle of puff pastry in a round baking tin (Ø 30cm), spread the almond mixture on top, leaving the rim free. Brush the rim with a little water and place the second slice of puff pastry on top and press it down well.

Leave to cool in the refrigerator for 1 hour, then brush with the egg yolk and carve a diamond-shaped pattern (approx. 4 cm side length) into the surface of the puff pastry with the tip of a knife.

Pierce the surface of the flat cake slightly in the middle so that the flat cake does not rise too much.

Bake in a preheated oven at 200°C for 25 minutes until golden brown.

Serve warm.

HEARTY TARTELETTES WITH APPLE

Working time approx. 15 minutes
cooking / baking time approx. 25 minutes
Total time approx. 40 minutes

Ingredients
3 slices of puff pastry, frozen
2 medium sized apples, sour
1 cup crème fraîche
2 medium spring onions, cut into rings
75 g bacon, diced
Oil
salt and pepper
Garlic

preparation
Defrost the puff pastry. Peel and core the apples and
cut them into small cubes. Cut the spring onions into
small rings.

Fry the onions, apples and bacon in a small pan in a

little oil, they should only brown slightly. Then let them cool down a bit, mix with crème fraîche and season with salt, pepper and a little garlic if you like. Cut the puff pastry sheets in half and line small muffin tins with them (works best if you cut the corners a little bit). Fill with the crème fraîche mixture.

Bake in a hot oven at 200 °C top/bottom heat for about 20 - 25 minutes.

Serve with a small salad and a cool Pinot Gris from Rheinhessen.

The above mentioned quantities result in 2 Tartelettes per person, this is a small main meal, as starter 1 Tartelette per person should be enough.

PICKLED OLIVES

Working time approx. 20 minutes
Rest period approx. 12 hours
Total time approx. 12 hours 20 minutes

Ingredients
4 clove garlic
1 piece of orange peel, untreated
4 sprigs thyme
4 sprigs rosemary
4 sprigs of basil
2 bay leaves, fresh, alternatively dried
1 chili pepper, red
150 g olives, black in brine
150 g olives, green in brine (if possible Picholines)
100 ml olive oil

Preparation
Peel the garlic and chop very finely, cut the orange peel very finely. Wash the herbs, shake dry and pluck from the stalks. Chop very finely with the bay leaf. Wash and clean the chili pepper and cut into fine rings.

Drain the olives and mix everything together. Marinate for at least 12 hours.

RILLETTES D'ANGERS

7246 kcal
Total time approx. 35 minutes

Ingredients
1 kg pork neck, roughly diced
500 g bacon, fat, diced
1 glass of water
salt and pepper
250 g lard
5 bay leaves

Preparation
Salt and pepper the meat cubes.

Melt the bacon cubes in a heavy pot until only greaves are left. Now add the meat, water and bay leaves, bring to the boil once and then simmer on a low heat for about 4-5 hours. The meat should now fall apart.

Either fill it hot into earthenware pots or into glasses, press the meat down a bit and let it cool down. If the fat layer is not high enough (it should be about 1/2 cm above the meat), melt lard and pour it over the meat.

Shelf life in the refrigerator is about 4 weeks. With me this is always much faster.

If you want to preserve the rillettes, you should fill them hot into glasses, pour lard over them, put a lid on it and boil down at 100°C for 45 minutes.
Make sure that the glasses are only filled to ¾.

HAM AND CHEESE TART

1241 kcal

Total time approx. 10 minutes

Ingredients
3 plates puff pastry, frozen
500 g cheese (Gouda)
200 g ham, cooked
50 g ham (smoked ham)
4 eggs
200 g cream
50 g crème fraîche
1 garlic clove
salt and pepper
Nutmeg

Preparation
Grease a springform pan with a diameter of 26-28 cm and line the bottom with 2 of the thawed puff pastry slices and the edge with one.

Finely grate the cheese, cut cooked ham and smoked

ham (alternatively, dried meat is also possible) into small cubes and press the garlic clove through.

Mix the cheese, eggs, cream, crème fraiche, garlic and spices well with a hand mixer to form a creamy mixture. Use salt very carefully and only a little.

Carefully fold in the diced cooked ham and smoked ham and pour the mixture into the prepared form.

Bake in the preheated oven at 180 degrees for 45-55 minutes, then leave to rest for 5 minutes, remove from the form and serve.

As main course we like to eat a green salad and baguette with it.

As a starter the amount is enough for 8 persons, because this dish is very filling.

TARTINES AU CHOCOLAT

Total time approx. 30 minutes

Ingredients
For the short pastry:
150 g butter
75 g powdered sugar
1 pinch of salt
225 g flour
75 g almond, ground
1 tablespoon of water
For the filling:
100 g butter
100 g dark chocolate
75 g sugar
125 g almond, ground
200 g walnuts, chopped
2 tablespoons cocoa powder
2 tablespoons of milk
chocolate, dark, for garnishing

Preparation

First, for the shortcrust pastry, stir the butter with powdered sugar and salt until foamy. Stir in the flour and almonds with the water, fold the dough into a ball with your hands and wrap in foil. Chill for about 1 hour.

For the filling, heat the butter with the chocolate in a water bath while stirring until the chocolate has melted. Pour into a mixing bowl, stir in sugar, almonds, walnuts, cocoa and finally the milk. Set aside.

Now roll out the short pastry between 2 layers of cling film about ½ cm thick to a rectangle. Cut the pastry sheet in half. Spread the chocolate filling on one half and place the other half on top.

Bake in the oven preheated to 160°C for 25-30 minutes, take out and let cool down. Then cut very carefully with a sharp knife into rectangles, lozenges or triangles. Decorate as desired with melted chocolate.

Leave to stand for at least one day in an airtight container so that the dough becomes nice and tender.

POPPY SEED PARFAIT WITH ORANGE SAUCE

Working time approx. 35 minutes
Rest period approx. 8 hours
Total time about 8 hours 35 minutes

Ingredients
For the parfait:
90 ml water
75 g sugar
3 egg yolks
250 ml cream
2 tablespoons poppy seed
1 pinch of cinnamon

For the sauce:
200 ml orange juice, freshly squeezed
2 teaspoons cornstarch
2 tablespoons of sugar
3 tablespoons orange liqueur

For decoration:

25 g dark chocolate
Fruit, as desired

Preparation
For the parfait:
In a small pot, briefly boil the water with the sugar. The sugar should dissolve completely. Remove from the heat and let it cool down until lukewarm.

Beat the egg yolks in a small bowl with the hand mixer for a few minutes at the highest setting until foamy.
Whip the cream until half stiff and set aside. Line small moulds or cups with aluminium foil and set aside.

Add the cooled sugar syrup to the egg yolk while stirring. Pour the mixture back into the pot and whisk over a simmering water bath for 4 - 5 minutes until creamy. The water should not touch the small pot. Then place the pot in a cold water bath, if necessary with ice cubes, and beat the mixture until cold. Meanwhile, add poppy seeds and cinnamon.
Carefully fold the cream into the egg yolk mixture and fill into the moulds.

Put the parfait in the freezer for at least 6 hours, but better overnight.
Before serving, place the plates briefly in the freezer.

For the sauce:
Squeeze oranges and mix the cornflour with some

orange juice.

Boil up the remaining orange juice in a small pot with the other ingredients and let it simmer briefly. Finally add the cornflour and let it thicken.

For the decoration:

Lay a piece of baking paper ready.

Melt the dark chocolate and let it cool down a bit. Pour the chocolate into a freezer bag and cut off a small corner. Use the piping bag to paint small grids on the baking paper and put the chocolate grids in the fridge.

Cut the fruits into small pieces and serve the parfait together with the chocolate grids and the sauce on the pre-cooled plates.

APPLE TART CLASSIC

2063 kcal
Working time approx. 25 minutes
Rest period approx. 1 hour
Total time approx. 1 hour 25 minutes

Ingredients
160 g flour
50 g powdered sugar, sieved
100 g butter, cold, in pieces
1 pinch of salt
1 egg yolk
2 apples, sourish
2 tablespoons lemon juice
2 tablespoons sugar, brown
Fat, for the mould

Preparation
Mix the flour with the powdered sugar, egg yolk, salt and pieces of butter to form a smooth dough ball. It is best to crush the butter firmly with your hands. Chill for 1 hour.

Roll out the dough thinly and put it into a greased tart tin (approx. 20-24 cm diameter). Press carefully in the edges of the form and cut off the excess at the edge.

Peel, quarter, core and cut the apples into 1 cm wide slices. Mix with 2 tablespoons lemon juice. Cover the dough with the apple slices like roof tiles and sprinkle with the brown sugar.

Bake the tart in the oven preheated to 200°C at top/bottom heat on the lowest rack for 30-35 minutes until golden brown.

LAVENDER CAKE

Total time approx. 15 minutes

Ingredients
1 cup of oil, (sunflower oil)
2 cups of sugar
3 cups of flour
4 eggs
1 package baking powder
1 package vanilla sugar
1 cup of sparkling mineral water
3 sprigs of lavender

Preparation
Mix the eggs with sugar and vanilla sugar until thick. Add oil and mineral water little by little. Mix flour with baking powder, sieve over it and mix in. Finally, fold in the plucked lavender flowers.
Grease a baking tray, spread the dough on it and bake at circulating air 150 degrees for about 25 minutes.
After cooling down, dust with powdered sugar and garnish with lavender flowers. Cut into pieces.

IMPRINT

Mindful Publishing
by
TTENTION Inc.
Wilmington - DE19806
Trolley Square 20c

Instagram: mindful_publishing
Contact: mindful.publishing@web.de

Printed in Great Britain
by Amazon